SCHOOL PRINCIPALS

Cindy Klingel and Robert B. Noyed

The Rourke Press, Inc.
Vero Beach, Florida 32964

PHOTO CREDITS
© Flanagan Publishing Services/Romie Flanagan

We would like to thank the students and staff of Channing Memorial
School for their valuable assistance in producing this book.

Library of Congress Cataloging-in-Publication Data

Klingel, Cynthia Fitterer.
    School principals / by Cindy Klingel and Robert B. Noyed.
        p. cm. — (School helpers)
    Includes index.
    Summary: Describes the school principal's day as she works with
students, parents, teachers, and other school workers.
        ISBN 1-57103-330-0
        1. School principals—Juvenile literature. 2. School management
and organization—Juvenile literature. [1. School principals.
2. Occupations.] I. Noyed, Robert B. II. Title.

LB283 1.9 .K45 2001
371.2'012 — dc21   99-059287
                                                          CIP

Printed in the USA

CONTENTS

About the Authors

Cindy Klingel has worked as a high school English teacher and an elementary teacher. She is currently the curriculum director for a Minnesota school district. Writing children's books is another way that continues her passion for sharing the written word with children. Cindy Klingel is a frequent visitor to the children's section of bookstores and enjoys spending time with her many friends, family, and two daughters.

Bob Noyed started his career as a newspaper reporter. Since then, he has worked in communications and public relations for more than fourteen years for a Minnesota school district. He enjoys writing books for children and finds that it brings a different feeling of challenge and accomplishment from other writing projects. He is an avid reader who also enjoys music, theater, travelling, and spending time with his wife, son, and daughter.

The person you know best at school is probably your teacher. But many other school helpers keep the school running. You may not know about all they do. Here are some of the many things your school principal does.

The principal is in charge of the school. This is a big responsibility. The principal works with students, parents, teachers, and other people who work in the school. The principal makes many decisions every day about the school.

The principal is responsible for the running of the school.

When students arrive in the morning, one of the people they see is the principal. She is often in the halls greeting students as they arrive. Many students have questions for the principal. Some students have stories to tell the principal.

The principal often starts the day talking to students on the playground.

It is important that students follow rules when they are at school. The principal helps to remind students of the rules. The principal likes to be involved with students in activities. Sometimes the principal has a **student council**. Those students on the council might work to do fun and interesting things.

Principals attend student council meetings.

Teachers and other people who work in the school depend on the principal for many things. They ask the principal for information. Sometimes they need the principal to help them with an important decision.

Principals often work with people from the community, such as police officers.

The principal spends time in classrooms. She wants to see what the teachers are teaching. She wants to understand what kinds of things students are learning. This will help her to be a better principal.

Visiting classrooms is an important part of a principal's day.

The principal often talks with parents. A parent may call the principal with a question. Sometimes a parent may call with a **concern**. There are also many parents and new families who visit the school during the day.

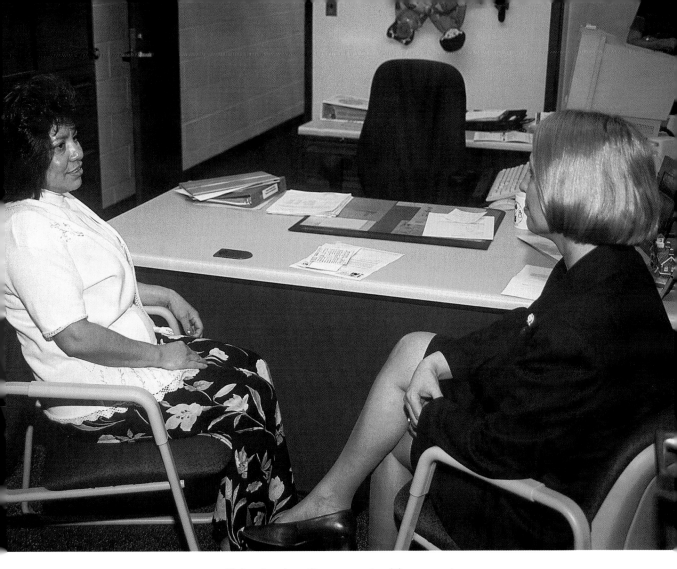

Principals often meet with parents.

The principal has many meetings with parents, too. There are usually formal meetings with a parent-teacher group. These meetings are often at night. At the meetings, the principal explains everything that is happening in the school. At the school's **open house**, the principal meets many parents!

At the school's open house, parents visit with teachers and the principal.

BC 15386

The principal talks often with the school's custodian. The principal needs to make sure everything is clean and working safely and properly.

Principals rely on many people to keep the school running.

The principal also has to spend time working in her office. There are many important papers to read and sign. The principal often does work in the office before the start of the school day and also after everyone goes home. There are also a lot of **professional** meetings for the principal to attend with other school principals.

When the school year ends, the principal still has much to do. She finishes reports about the year that has just ended. She also prepares for fall, when everyone returns for a new school year. There's always something for the principal to do!

Principals use computers to help them get things done.

FURTHER INFORMATION

Books

Boraas, Tracey. *School Principals*. Mankato, Minn.: Capstone
 Press, 1999.
Thaler, Michael, and Jared Lee. *Principal from the Black Lagoon*.
 New York: Scholastic, 1993.

Web Sites
American School Directory

http://www.asd.com/
Locate your own school's web site.

Being a principal is a big job.

GLOSSARY

concern (con SERN) — a worry

open house (O pen HOWSE) — a special event for parents to visit a school and speak with teachers and the principal

professional (pro FESH un al) — related to career

student council (STOO dent COWN suhl) — a group of students who organize school events and make decision about school life

INDEX